People of
Virginia

Karla Smith

Heinemann Library
Chicago, Illinois

Designed by Heinemann Library
Page layout by Wilkinson Design
Photo research by Kathy Creech
Printed and bound in the United States by Lake
Book Manufacturing, Inc.

07 06 05 04 03
10 9 8 7 6 5 4 3 2 1

**Library of Congress
Cataloging-in-Publication Data**
Smith, Karla, 1947-
   People of Virginia / by Karla Smith.
      p. cm. -- (Heinemann state studies)
Summary: Examines the diversity of people who
inhabit the state of Virginia, beginning with the
Native Americans.
Includes bibliographical references and index.
   ISBN 1-40340-359-7 -- ISBN 1-40340-581-6
(pbk.)
   1. Virginia--History--Juvenile literature. 2.
Virginia--Population--Juvenile literature. 3.
Ethnology--Virginia--Juvenile literature. 4.
Virginia--Biography--Juvenile literature. [1. Virginia-
-Population. 2. Ethnology--Virginia. 3. Virginia--
Biography. 4. Indians of North America--Virginia.]
I. Title. II. Series.
   F226.3 .S654 2003
   305.8'009755--dc21

2002152999

Acknowledgments
The author and publishers are grateful to the
following for permission to reproduce copyright
material: title page (L-R) AP Wide World Photo,
Bettmann/Corbis, Pace Gregory/Corbis SYGMA;
contents page (L-R) Bettmann/Corbis, Ariel Skel-
ley/Corbis, White House Collection, Courtesy
White House Historical Association; p. 4 Ariel Skel-
ley/Corbis; p. 9 Farrell Grehan/Corbis; pp. 10, 15,
18, 20R, 22, 24, 29, 32B, 33B, 34T, 36, 38T. 38B,
39, 40T, 41 Bettmann/Corbis; pp. 11, 32T, 40B
Alex Brandon/Heinemann Library; pp. 12, 13B, 42,
44T Corbis; p. 13T Lee Snider/Corbis; p. 14 Larry
Luxner; p. 17 Kevin Fleming/Corbis; pp. 19, 21B,
44B The Granger Collection, New York; pp. 20L,
38C Burstein Collection/Corbis; pp. 21T, 40C
Library of Congress; p. 26T The Image Bank/Getty
Images; pp. 26B, 35B AP Wide World Photo; p. 28
Virginia Historical Society; p. 30 Joseph
Sohm/ChromoSohm Inc./Corbis; p. 31 Paul Con-
klin/PhotoEdit; p. 33T Mitchell Gerber/Corbis; p.
34B Pace Gregory/Corbis SYGMA; p. 35T Tim
Wright/Corbis; p. 43 White House Collection,
Courtesy White House Historical Association

Cover photographs by (row L-R) Bettmann/Corbis,
Alex Brandon/Heinemann Library, Bettmann/Cor-
bis, Alex Brandon/Heinemann Library; (main)
Omni Photo Communications Inc./Index Stock
Imagery

Special thanks to Jean Hodges for her expert
advice on the series.

Every effort has been made to contact copyright
holders of any material reproduced in this book.
Any omissions will be rectified in subsequent
printings if notice is given to the publisher.

Some words are shown in bold, **like this.**
You can find out what they mean by looking
in the glossary.

Contents

Virginia's People

The people of Virginia have a long history. All people who have lived in Virginia, from the nomads of 20,000 years ago to the communities of today, have shaped the state and created its history. Virginia has been home to leaders of our nation's government, famous athletes, important educators, writers, artists, and more. Virginia's people have led the way in creating a nation.

Virginia is home to people of many different backgrounds. Some come from families of immigrants, while other families have always lived in the United States. People of all **cultures** *like to celebrate at festivals that honor their* **traditions.**

VIRGINIA'S CENSUS DATA

Virginia reached a population of 1,000,000 residents in 1830. Since then, the population has continued to grow rapidly. The 2000 U.S. **Census** counted 7,078,515 residents in the state of Virginia. Virginia experienced huge population

Virginia's Demographics: 1990 vs. 2000

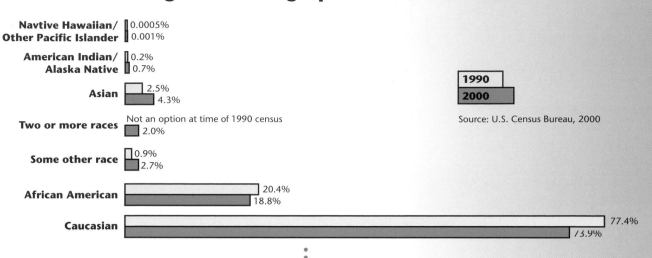

Navtive Hawaiian/Other Pacific Islander: 0.0005% (1990), 0.001% (2000)

American Indian/Alaska Native: 0.2% (1990), 0.7% (2000)

Asian: 2.5% (1990), 4.3% (2000)

Two or more races: Not an option at time of 1990 census, 2.0% (2000)

Some other race: 0.9% (1990), 2.7% (2000)

African American: 20.4% (1990), 18.8% (2000)

Caucasian: 77.4% (1990), 73.9% (2000)

Source: U.S. Census Bureau, 2000

growth between 1990 and 2000. Each and every day between 1990 and 2000, Virginia added about 200 people. Virginia is the 12th ranked state in population in the United States.

*Virginia's mix of cultures became more **diverse** during the years between 1990 and 2000.*

Today, nearly 73 out of 100 of Virginia's people are of European **descent.** Most of the rest are African American, serving as a reminder of the important role that African slaves had in the development of the state.

The 2000 U.S. Census recorded 570,279 foreign-born residents in Virginia—8 percent of the state's entire population. Between 1990 and 2000, Virginia's **immigrant** population almost doubled. Many of Virginia's new residents have settled in northern Virginia. Over half of these new Virginians have come from Asian countries, such as Korea, Vietnam, India, and the Philippines. Others arrived from the United Kingdom, Canada, Peru, El Salvador, the Dominican Republic, Germany, and Mexico. Recently, Virginia has also seen a wave of immigration from Iran, Pakistan, and the former Soviet Union.

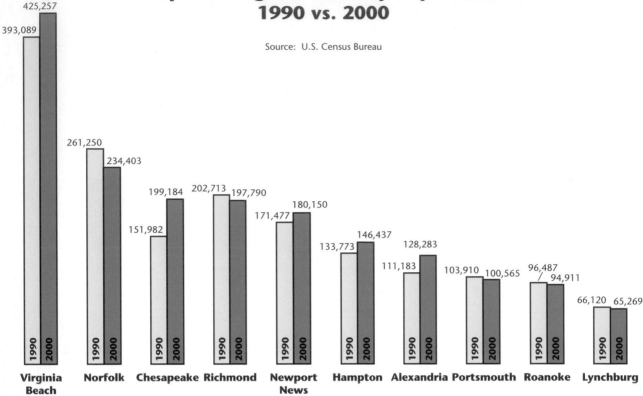

Top Ten Virginia Cities by Population
1990 vs. 2000

Source: U.S. Census Bureau

City	1990	2000
Virginia Beach	393,089	425,257
Norfolk	261,250	234,403
Chesapeake	151,982	199,184
Richmond	202,713	197,790
Newport News	171,477	180,150
Hampton	133,773	146,437
Alexandria	111,183	128,283
Portsmouth	103,910	100,565
Roanoke	96,487	94,911
Lynchburg	66,120	65,269

The ten biggest cities of Virginia vary widely in population. For instance, Virginia Beach, the biggest city, is nearly double the size of the next biggest city, Norfolk.

WHERE DO THE PEOPLE OF VIRGINIA LIVE?

Virginia has 95 counties, 189 towns, and 40 cities. About three out of every four people in Virginia live in one of the eight **metropolitan** areas. Five of these metropolitan areas lie completely within Virginia: Charlottesville, Danville, Lynchburg, Richmond-Petersburg, and Roanoke. The Norfolk-Virginia Beach-Newport News area, also known as Hampton Roads, crosses the border into North Carolina. Five of Virginia's counties and five of its cities extend into the Washington, D.C., metropolitan area as well. Nine of the ten largest cities in Virginia are either along the Atlantic coast or along the **fall line.**

No matter where people in Virginia live, the state is rich in history and **cultural diversity.** Every resident contributes to making Virginia a great place to live.

First People, Early Settlers

During the last **Ice Age,** thick sheets of ice buried much of present-day North America. A **land bridge** stretched across the Bering Strait, which now separates Asia from Alaska. Scientists believe that about 40,000 years ago, people began to move from what is now Asia across the land bridge and became the first people to reach what we now call the North American continent. Virginia was not covered in ice, so people were able to settle here.

By 1600, there were about 40 groups of Native Americans in Virginia, totaling about 20,000 people. The Powhatans are the best-known Virginia native

Virginia's first inhabitants were several Native American tribes belonging to three language groups: Iroquoian, Siouan, and Algonquian.

Three Language Groups

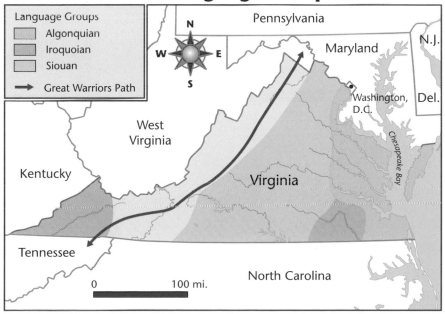

Language Groups
- Algonquian
- Iroquoian
- Siouan
- → Great Warriors Path

Pennsylvania

Maryland

N.J.

Washington, D.C.

Del.

West Virginia

Kentucky

Virginia

Chesapeake Bay

Tennessee

North Carolina

0   100 mi.

peoples because of their contact—and conflicts—with the English settlers. By 1607, when the English settlers arrived in Virginia, there were about 161 Powhatan villages. Their **tradition** stated that they had been in Virginia for 300 years, but it may have been as long as 1,500 years. The most powerful chief in Virginia was Powhatan.

Within 160 years after the Europeans came, the Native American groups of Virginia had almost disappeared. The settlers and Native Americans did not always have a good relationship. They disagreed about how land should be owned. The native peoples wanted the land for keeping their **cultural** independence. The English needed the land to fulfill the promise of money that had drawn them here.

Eventually, wars with colonists and European diseases destroyed most of the native tribes. The surviving Native Americans were driven from the land by 1700. Out of an original 40 tribes, today only eight are recognized by the Commonwealth of Virginia. These include the Chickahominy, the Eastern Chickahominy, the Mattaponi, the Upper Mattaponi, the Monacan, the Nansemond, the Pamunkey, and the Rappahannock. There are also several other tribes in the process of seeking recognition from the

Thomas Hariot

Much of what we know about Virginia's early native residents comes from a report written in 1588 by a man named Thomas Hariot. Hariot's report, called *A Brief and True Report of the New Found Land of Virginia,* was based on the time he spent living on Roanoke Island. In it, he writes that the local Native Americans " ... **bade** us welcome. Then they brought us to their village in the land called Roanoac, and unto their ... prince, [who] entertained us with ... **courtesy** ... Such was our arrival into the part of the world which we call Virginia...."

Powhatan: A Powerful Chief

Years before English settlers came to Jamestown, Powhatan was the chief of six tribes. By 1607, Powhatan and his warriors had conquered 32 tribes between the Potomac and James Rivers. Powhatan ruled by force. He was so powerful that tribes paid him a tax, or **tribute.** Tribes brought corn, deer, tobacco, and other goods to Powhatan in return for protection. When the English arrived in Virginia, Powhatan was the most powerful chief in the area. Powhatan's tribes attacked the settlers many times. The English also attacked the tribes. Powhatan's power was slowly taken over by wave after wave of new settlers.

U.S. government. The Pamunkey and Mattaponi **reservations** are the two oldest Indian reservations in the United States.

WHO WERE THE SETTLERS?

Many of the first **immigrants** to arrive in early Virginia in the 1600s were poor. Many had been out of work in England. They came as **indentured servants.** Indentured servants were people who signed a contract agreeing to work for someone else for several years in exchange for their **passage** to Virginia. They were given food, clothing, and shelter during this time. At the end of the indenture, many were given a few acres of land. However, half of them died before their service was completed. One out of four remained poor afterward.

Settlers in Virginia built houses that were much like the houses in England. They often built row houses, which are similar

The Adam Thoroughgood House is one of the oldest brick homes in the United States.

New settlers arriving in Jamestown were faced with many new challenges. They needed to learn to farm, gather resources, and use the land in order to survive.

to apartment buildings. The Adam Thoroughgood House, located in Virginia Beach, is one of the best examples of an English house built in the 1600s. Within a few years, settlers also built windmills, water mills, taverns, guesthouses, churches, and mansions to match those they knew from home. By 1619, twelve years after the colony at Jamestown was established, there were eleven settlements in Virginia along the James River.

Each ship that arrived in Virginia brought more English settlers. They brought their language, clothing, religion, and **traditions** with them. They gave English names to new settlements, such as Hampton and Norfolk. Many places and rivers were named after the royal families of England. The James River was named for King James I. The College of William and Mary, King and Queen County, Prince Edward County, Prince William County, and Charles City were all named in honor of the British royal family.

AFRICANS IN EARLY VIRGINIA

In 1619, a new group of people was brought to Jamestown. A Dutch ship landed with Africans captured from the Spanish. These were the first known Africans to live in British North America. The captain of the ship traded these prisoners for food. Some historians think the Africans were **indentured servants.** They might have become free after a number of years of work.

This is a replica of the ship Godspeed that brought settlers, and possibly indentured servants, to the colonies.

The Africans arrived at an important time in Virginia's history. Previously, English indentured servants had provided all labor necessary to work in the tobacco fields. As the tobacco business grew, however, planters discovered that they needed more workers. As the African population in Virginia grew—by 1650 there were between 300 and 500 Africans—records indicated that the majority were considered to be slaves, and that few were thought to be indentured servants. The difference between them was that slaves could not gain their freedom and indentured servants only had to work for a certain amount of time to pay back their **passage.** In 1650, Virginia passed a law stating that white indentured servants could buy their freedom. Black servants could not—they automatically became slaves.

By 1776, the African slaves made up 40 percent of the population. Slaves on **plantations** were often not allowed to learn to read and write. They often lived in small, windowless cabins with dirt floors and no furniture. Slaves worked from sunrise to sunset, grinding corn, milking cows, butchering meat, growing vegetables, and washing and mending clothes. Slave women were as likely as men to be sent into the fields to work.

Cash Crop

In 1612, a Jamestown settler named John Rolfe planted some tobacco seeds he had brought from the Caribbean islands. The tobacco grew easily in this new land. This new kind of Virginia tobacco became very popular in England. Virginia settlers finally had a product from which they could make money.

Tobacco wore out the land quickly, however. A planter could only use the same field for about three years in a row. As the fields in the Tidewater lands wore out, planters began to move west and forced Native Americans from their land. In 1643, four **forts** were built on the **fall line** to protect settlers from angry Native Americans. The forts became important trading posts.

Despite a very hard life, the slaves kept their African **cultures** alive. Various African cultural **traditions,** including food and cooking preferences, music, dance, vocabulary, religious and healing practices, and folklore mixed to form a new Virginian African-American culture that strongly affected white culture as well.

Virginian African Americans are also known for their spirituals. Spirituals are considered one of the beginnings of American music. Slaves sang songs while they worked. They sometimes passed coded messages to each other in songs. Many songs helped travelers on the **Underground Railroad.** "Follow the Drinking

Slaves were never given easy jobs. In this picture, slaves are working to fill barrels with tobacco. Four white men are supervising their work.

Many of the small one- and two-room houses intended for slaves were poorly built and often were not even sealed to keep the weather out.

Gourd" was a song that passed on information about hiding places for escaping slaves. The "drinking gourd" referred to the North Star, which pointed the way to freedom in the North. These songs are still sung today, and teach new generations of Virginians about African-American history.

Booker T. Washington

From 1895 until his death in 1915, Booker T. Washington was the nation's dominant African-American leader. Born in 1856, in Franklin County, Virginia, Washington was a slave. He was freed after the Civil War, and helped to support his family by working in salt and coal mines. Washington taught himself the alphabet and went to school at night. When he was sixteen, he walked to the Hampton Normal and Agricultural Institute, which had been established to educate former slaves. To gain admission into the school, he worked by sweeping and dusting a classroom, and he was able to earn his food and room by working as a janitor.

After graduation, Washington became the principal of a training school for African Americans in Tuskegee, Alabama. The school, Tuskegee Institute, became a major center of **industrial** training for African-American youths. Washington urged white business owners to employ African-American laborers. He called on African Americans to concentrate on earning more money and improving their lives. He believed that their need to earn a decent living called for training in crafts and trades. In an effort to encourage the growth of African-American businesses, Washington also organized the National Negro Business League in 1900.

Cultural Groups of Virginia

New groups of **immigrants** from Europe eventually joined English settlers in the Piedmont and Valley areas. French, German, and Scotch–Irish settlers came to Virginia in the early 1700s.

FRENCH HUGUENOTS

In 1700, the ship *Mary Ann* brought 207 Huguenots to Virginia. They had been **exiled** from their villages in France because of their **Protestant** religion. King Louis XIV of France had decided that Protestants would no longer be able to worship in his country. The king of England invited the Huguenots to the colony of Virginia.

The Huguenot settlers, who were mostly **artisans,** had to learn quickly how to farm. The first winter was hard for the French settlers. Their supplies ran out, so the English governor helped them with food donations from English colonists. In a few years, however, these new Virginians were growing fruit, making wine, weaving cloth, and raising cattle along the James River. They traded goods with

The Virginia governor, Francis Howard of Effingham, promised that the Huguenots could have their own ministers, rather than be required to attend English services.

the Native Americans who remained in the area. Huguenots also started farms along other rivers in the Piedmont. The houses they built were similar to houses found in France. Double front doors, or "French doors," were part of many Piedmont houses near Monacan Town.

GERMANS COME TO VIRGINIA

In 1714, Governor Alexander Spotswood brought German iron miners into Virginia. Spotswood's plan was to start an iron-making **industry** on land he owned in Virginia. He also wanted to extend settlement into Piedmont. These new immigrants mined for iron **ore** and made iron tools. By 1720, the Germans' settlement had become the **county seat** of Spotsylvania County.

In the 1730s, more German immigrants came to Virginia. This particular group of Germans was eager to come to the colonies because of war, **famine,** and religious **persecution** in their homeland. Virginia offered them religious freedom if they settled here. They walked south along the **Great Wagon Road** from Pennsylvania to settle towns such as Winchester, Strasburg, and Harrisonburg. They were excellent farmers. They built homes made from limestone and fieldstone. These homes later became known as Pennsylvania-style houses.

Many more Germans immigrated to Virginia in the following years. In fact, so many Germans came that by 1790, 28 percent of Virginia's Caucasian population was German-speaking. Some German immigrants opened inns and taverns for

Alexander Spotswood

Mysteries and Melungeons

As these new groups of settlers moved west through the Blue Ridge Mountains in the 1700s, they were surprised to find some families already living there. Those families spoke a blend of Spanish and Old English, which they called Portyghee. Some thought these people were Native Americans. Others thought they were escaped slaves who had married Native Americans. Still others believed that they were the **descendants** of the members of the Lost Colony. Legends and stories about these people were told for years. They became known as Melungeons.

Today, most people believe that the Melungeons were really the descendants of many different groups of people, including Portuguese, Turks, Moors, Sephardic Jews, Africans, Native Americans, and Spaniards. Many Melungeons have moved and settled in the Allegheny Mountains. The name Allegheny actually comes from the Turkish words *Allah genis,* which means "God's vastness." Virginia's Melungeons add another interesting element to Virginia's **culture.**

travelers on the **Great Wagon Road.** They served foods from their homeland, such as yeast breads, sauerkraut, liverwurst, scrapple, pig's knuckles, and apple butter.

THE SCOTCH–IRISH MOVE TO THE VALLEY

The Scotch–Irish were people who were originally from Scotland, but had been living in Ireland. During the 1600s, many Scotch-Irish **immigrants** moved to Pennsylvania, seeking religious freedom. Most were **Presbyterians,** and were not permitted to practice their religion in Ireland. When these immigrants found that most of Pennsylvania's best farmland had been settled, they began looking at Virginia's Shenandoah Valley. In 1689, a law was passed in Virginia that allowed people to worship as they chose.

County fairs in Virginia often feature different kinds of music that reflect Virginia's culture. This bluegrass band plays in front of the Loudon County Courthouse in Leesburg.

In the 1730s, the Scotch-Irish traveled south and west into Virginia's **fertile** valleys. They introduced much of their culture to the colony. Perhaps most well-known was their fiddle music, called bluegrass music today.

The large movements of people into Virginia in the 1700s made it a society where people of **diverse ethnicities** and religions had to learn to get along. The idea of **toleration** became the new American ideal of freedom. These ideas are what began the American Revolution, helping the colonies break free of British rule.

Virginians in Government

In the 1770s, there was unrest in the colonies about who had the right to rule. Britain believed the colonies were theirs to control, while the colonists wanted to build their own system of government. Virginia's people were highly involved in trying to resolve this issue. By 1775, most Virginians did not believe that Britain could rule them from across the ocean.

"Give Me Liberty, or Give Me Death!"

Patrick Henry's parents were **immigrants** from Scotland. Patrick was born in 1736, in Hanover County, Virginia. He grew up in the newly settled Piedmont region. He loved the outdoors, horseback riding, and hunting, but did not like school. He went to work when he was 15 years old, but could not find a job that he liked. He tried both

running a store and being a farmer, but those jobs didn't work out. The two things that Patrick Henry liked to do most were read and talk. He read as many books about famous people and governments as he could find. He decided to become a lawyer, so he studied law books by himself. Patrick was a great speaker and won many cases. He also began to speak out about English taxes and laws. In a famous speech of 1775, Patrick Henry spoke what would become his most famous quote while debating American freedom from British control: "Give me liberty, or give me death!"

Virginian Signatures

The following Virginians signed the Declaration of Independence:

Richard Henry Lee

George Wythe

Benjamin Harrison

Thomas Jefferson

Carter Braxton

Thomas Nelson Jr.

Francis Lightfoot Lee

Virginia men like Thomas Jefferson and George Wythe studied the governments of the ancient Greeks and Romans. They knew what was needed to make a strong state and country. They were part of the **Continental Congress** that met in Philadelphia, Pennsylvania, in 1776. During this meeting, the Congress decided to become independent from Britain.

Thomas Jefferson had a tremendous role in shaping the U.S. government. He is sometimes called the founder of the **Democratic** party. During the meeting of the Continental Congress in 1776, Jefferson was asked to write the Declaration of Independence. His words became the basis upon which the new United States government was built. The right to life, liberty, and the pursuit of happiness are still part of our government today. Jefferson became the governor of Virginia in 1779, then the minister to France in 1785. In 1796, he took office as the vice president of the United States, leading to his election in 1801 as the third president of the United States.

Jefferson served two terms as president before retiring in 1809. He spent his final years tending his land, reading, writing, and spending time with family and friends. In 1819, he established the University of Virginia at Charlottesville. Jefferson died on July 4, 1826, exactly 50 years after the Declaration of Independence was adopted.

George Washington was also one of the representatives for Virginia at the Continental Congress meetings. When fighting broke out in the colonies between the colonists and the British, Washington was commander in chief of the Continental Army for the colonies. Through several long years of battle, his army defeated the British and won independence for the colonists in 1781. During the meeting of the Constitutional Convention in 1789, Washington was chosen as the first president of the new United States of America.

James Madison

THE VIRGINIAN DYNASTY

The third, fourth, and fifth presidents of the United States were also Virginians. Each contributed to the nation's **legacy.** While in office as the third president, Thomas Jefferson doubled the size of the country with the **Louisiana Purchase** of 1803. The fourth president, James Madison, kept Britain from taking American lands during the War of 1812. As the fifth president, James Monroe built roads, canals, and many **forts** to protect the nation from invasion from other countries.

James Monroe

THE CIVIL WAR AND VIRGINIA'S PEOPLE (1861–1865)

The state of Virginia and its people were deeply involved in the Civil War. Virginia was part of the Confederacy, which wanted to **secede** from the Union states of the North. Virginia's General Robert E. Lee led the largest Confederate army in many successful battles that gave hope to the people of the south. However, the North was able to conquer in the end, having better supplies and more men to fight.

Despite losing the war, Lee was the hero of the southern states. He set a good example by accepting defeat and spoke to the people about peace and national **unity.** Lee accepted the presidency of Washington College at Lexington, Virginia, in 1865. He believed it was his duty to guide the youth of the south in the years after the war. Lee established the School of Law, encouraged the study of sciences, and began programs in business instruction that led to the founding of the School of **Commerce** in 1906. After Lee's death in 1870, the name of the school was changed from Washington College to Washington and Lee University.

Robert E. Lee

The Civil War affected Virginia's people in very dramatic ways. Thirty-five counties west of the Appalachian Mountains split from Virginia in 1863 and became the state of West Virginia. Suddenly, people who had lived in Virginia their whole lives found themselves living in an entirely new state. Civil War battles destroyed the **plantation economy** in Virginia.

Maggie Walker

People faced tough times after the Civil War, but many of them, including newly freed African Americans, tried to find new opportunities. In 1867, a little girl named Maggie was born in Richmond. Her mother, Elizabeth Mitchell, had been a slave but was free when Maggie was born. Maggie went to public school in Richmond. She became a schoolteacher and later worked for the poor people in Richmond. In 1903, she helped open a bank called St. Luke Penny Savings Bank. This bank helped many African Americans start businesses and buy homes. She was the first woman bank president in the United States.

The lives of Virginia's farmers changed because of Cyrus McCormick. Born near Staunton, he built a machine called a reaper that harvested wheat much faster than by hand. Thanks to the reaper, the valleys of Virginia became known as the "Breadbasket of the South."

Plantations were burned and fields were abandoned. Many planters who went to fight in the war had nothing left when they returned home. The factories in Richmond and Petersburg were destroyed, too.

POST-WAR LIFE (1865–1900)

The **Emancipation Proclamation** in 1863 had freed the slaves in the southern states that were rebelling against the Union. Many freed slaves left Virginia and traveled North, looking for work. Many who stayed in Virginia became sharecroppers. A sharecropper raised part of a landowner's crop and was paid a share of the profit from its sale. However, if the crop was poor, the sharecropper got nothing and had to obtain permission from the landowner to work another season. Most sharecroppers ended up in **debt.**

After the Civil War, the Thirteenth Amendment freed all U.S. slaves, no matter where they were. During the years after the war, African American and white teachers from the north and south, **missionary** organizations, churches, and schools worked to give the freed population the opportunity to learn. Former slaves were eager to learn how to read and write.

Virginians struggled to recover from the Civil War. Many moved from the ruined farms to the cities, looking for work. Factories opened in most major cities during the early 1880s. **Textiles,** furniture, and chemicals were products **exported** from Virginia. While many people moved to cities looking for factory jobs, tobacco again became Virginia's largest **agricultural** export. Newport News opened one of the country's largest shipyards. Thousands of workers also found jobs in Chesapeake Bay fisheries and seafood processing plants.

In the late 1800s, railroads connected cities to markets in the North. Small towns such as Gladstone and Big Stone Gap sprang up along railroad lines. In 1881, Big Lick had a population of 400. The railroad transformed a small town into present-day Roanoke, with a population of 25,000 in 1892. Roanoke became the home of the Norfolk & Western Railway. Beginning in 1838, with a nine-mile line from Petersburg, Virginia, to City Point, Virginia, the Norfolk & Western grew to a system serving 14 states and a province of Canada on more than 7,000 miles of road.

Freedmen's Bureau

The Bureau of Refugees, Freedmen, and Abandoned Lands was established in 1865. The bureau was created to assist all the newly freed slaves in getting food, medicine, and clothing. The bureau also established over 1,000 schools for African Americans. All major African-American colleges in the United States were either funded by or received money from the bureau. The bureau was discontinued in 1872 due to a lack of government support.

Virginians in the 20th Century

When the new century began, it brought new hope to the people of Virginia. During this time, Virginia experienced its greatest population growth in an area called the Urban Corridor. The Urban Corridor extends south from Washington, D.C., through Arlington, Alexandria, and Richmond. It then continues southeast to the Hampton Roads area—Newport News, Hampton, Norfolk, Virginia Beach, and Portsmouth. Some cities in this corridor are close to Washington, D.C., where the federal government employs many workers. Others are close to Virginia's many ports and shipbuilding **industries,** which depend on access to water. All are centers of trade, transportation, and industry.

JIM CROW LAWS

However, life was not good for all of Virginia's people. In 1901, the Jim Crow laws were passed. Named after a song from the 1820s that made fun of African

The Jim Crow laws said that African Americans in the South were only allowed to use specially-marked drinking fountains.

Americans, the Jim Crow laws enforced **segregation.** These laws were made to give power back to white people. The laws forced African Americans to ride separate buses, eat at separate restaurants, use separate bathrooms, and even drink from separate water fountains from those used by white people. Although these separate facilities were supposed to be equal, they rarely were. The places used by white people were usually far better. These laws were designed to **discriminate** against African Americans.

A New, Unfair State Constitution

In 1902, specially elected **delegates** held a meeting to write a new state constitution. In this new state constitution, all voters had to pay a tax of $6.00 in order to vote. Since most African Americans could not afford to pay the fee, they could not vote. Also, a test was given at the polls that asked about Virginia's constitution. These tests were used to keep African Americans from voting. Election official also sometimes pretended that African Americans were not on the list of voters. Some African Americans were even beaten or threatened with the loss of their jobs when they tried to vote. As a result of these unfair practices, half of Virginia's men, both African Americans and poor whites, lost voting rights. Women at this time did not have the right to vote at all.

Virginia Becomes a Military Center

The United States was involved in two world wars during the 20th century. Preparing for war helped

Virginia Military Institute

The Virginia Military Institute has trained many war officers. Virginia was a training ground for 45,000 troops during World War I. Norfolk became the headquarters for the Atlantic Fleet of the United States Navy. Quantico became the headquarters of the United States Marine Corps.

Female factory workers did all the same jobs as men during both world wars.

Virginia change from a rural state to an urban one and increased the amount of money coming into the state. The Urban Corridor areas needed thousands of workers to meet the war demands. At that time, many people moved to the Hampton Roads area from North Carolina and West Virginia to help with the war efforts.

WORLD WAR I (1914–1918)

Woodrow Wilson, a Virginia-born U.S. president, led the nation as a member of the **Allies** during World War I. Virginians were happy to fill the jobs created by the huge **guncotton** plant at Hopewell and the growth of the nation's largest naval base at Norfolk. However, they also were saddened by the loss of 2,500 Virginians who gave their lives as soldiers.

During World War I, women worked in offices and factories, filling in for the men who had gone to war. When the war was over, some women stopped working,

The Nineteenth Amendment to the Constitution gave women in the U.S. the right to vote in 1920. However, Virginia did not add the amendment to its state constitution until 1952.

but many single women continued with their jobs. Many people now felt that women should be able to vote and have the same political rights as men.

Virginians such as Lila Meade Valentine and Ellen Glasgow helped start the Equal **Suffrage** League. This group later joined the League of Women Voters, a national organization that fought for women's rights.

Virginia's War Heroes

Many of the most famous commanders of World War II were native Virginians or had strong ties to the state. Among them were George C. Marshall, Alexander Archer Vandegrift, Lemuel C. Shepherd, Lewis Burwell Puller, Douglas MacArthur, and George S. Patton Jr.

•George Catlett Marshall was the U.S. Army chief of staff throughout World War II. He took the seventeenth largest army in the world in 1939 and built it up to 8,000,000 men in 1945. Although born in Pennsylvania, Marshall came from a leading family of Virginia's Northern Neck, was a graduate of Virginia Military Institute, lived at **Fort** Myer during the war, and chose Leesburg for his retirement. Featured six times on the cover of *TIME*—twice as Man of the Year—Marshall was called the organizer of victory by British Prime Minister Winston Churchill. Marshall also won the Nobel Peace Prize in 1953.

•Lewis Burwell "Chesty" Puller of West Point, Virginia, attended Virginia Military Institute and led the First Marine Division at Peleliu in the Pacific. He retired as the Marine with the most honors in history.

•George S. Patton Jr., a native Californian, had Virginians on both sides of his family. He began his military career at Virginia Military Institute before transferring to West Point in New York. During World War II, his advances across France and Germany contributed greatly to the Allied victory.

Norfolk Naval Base provided very important supplies to the U.S. military during World War II.

In August of 1920, all of the women's hard work paid off. The Nineteenth Amendment was finally passed. Although some women already had the right to vote in several western states, this amendment guaranteed all women in the U.S. the right to vote in both state and national elections.

WORLD WAR II (1939–1945)

Even though the United States went through a severe **depression** in the 1930s, Virginia's people were not as affected because of the government and military jobs available here. When the U.S. entered World War II in 1941, Virginians were ready. People of Virginia participated in nearly every aspect of World War II. Its soldiers fought across the Pacific with the 29th Infantry Division. Virginia citizens built aircraft carriers, destroyers, submarines, and bombs. Virginians on the coast stood guard in watch towers, patrolled beaches, and watched for airplanes. The war came close to home in 1942 when German U-Boats sunk **Allied** ships at the opening of the Chesapeake Bay in Virginia.

During World War II, thousands of soldiers trained at the Norfolk Naval Base. The number of employees at the base grew by more than ten times. In 1939, there were 13,000 workers in the shipbuilding **industry** in Newport News. By 1943, there were 70,000. Virginia's **agricultural** industry also grew rapidly. The United States needed lots of food to feed its soldiers all over the world. It also needed many people to work the farms.

The Civil Rights Movement

Hundreds of African Americans from Virginia risked their lives for their country in World War I and II, just like white Virginians. They traveled and saw the world. They saw instances where people of different skin color could live together in mutual respect and **equality.** In World War II, African Americans fought to free the Jewish people who were being killed. Returning home to Virginia, the African Americans realized that they too were being punished for being different, and that was unfair. The African Americans were angry they did not have the same rights as the whites. They began to protest against the unfair treatment.

Equal Rights for All?

In May 1954, a court case called *Brown vs. Topeka Board of Education* was heard by the United States Supreme Court. It ruled that **segregation** in public schools was illegal. The Supreme Court demanded that all schools be **integrated.**

Harry F. Byrd Sr.

Many Virginians were angry about the Supreme Court's decision to end segregation and require integration. Many people believed that African Americans were not as good as white people. Many white people did not want their children to go to school with African-American children.

People were also against the Supreme Court decision because they felt that education should be controlled by the states themselves, not the federal government. Harry Byrd Sr., a United States senator from Virginia, led the movement in Virginia against integration. He used a technique called massive resistance to protest the Supreme Court's decision. This meant that schools that integrated would not get state funding.

In 1958, the Virginia government declared that no **integrated** school would receive money from the state. The Supreme Court had ordered Warren County schools to integrate, but Virginia's governor, J. Lindsay Almond Jr., ordered the schools to shut down. A week later, Charlottesville and Norfolk schools were also shut down. The next year, all the schools in Prince Edward County were shut down. As a result, many white and African-American children were unable to get an education.

Finally, Governor Almond and Harry Byrd lost the battle. People realized that the situation had to change. The Virginia State Assembly declared that the state could no longer shut down schools. By the mid 1960s, most of Virginia's schools had been integrated, and schools that once were only attended by white students now also accepted African-American students. In 1964, the Civil Rights Act was passed into law by President Lyndon B. Johnson. It guaranteed equal rights for all people, no matter what their race, sex, or religion.

This mother and daughter are originally from Pakistan, and now live in Virginia.

NEW IMMIGRANTS COME TO VIRGINIA

Immigrants fleeing problems in Europe during and after World War II (1939–1945) moved into many cities in Virginia during the 1940s and 1950s. Cuban refugees came to Virginia in the 1960s. After the Vietnam War (1964–1975), Virginia also welcomed people from the Southeast Asian countries of South Vietnam and

Cambodia. Today, Norfolk has one of the nation's largest Filipino communities. Northern Virginia has the largest Vietnamese population on the East Coast. Northern Virginia is also home to large communities of Hispanics and Koreans.

PEOPLE OF VIRGINIA TODAY

The Commonwealth of Virginia was shaped by the contributions of the people who came here from many different places. Virginians have shared their customs and history with each other and influenced the United States as a whole. African Americans, Greeks, Native Americans, Italians, Latinos, Filipinos, and many other groups hold fairs, festivals, dances, and art shows to celebrate and preserve their **cultures.** The state's long and important history is remembered and celebrated while Virginians look toward a bright future. Today, the values of representative government and the rights and freedoms that have been gained through the years are given to every Virginian from every cultural background. Virginia's **diverse** population will continue to add to the state's success and progress for many years to come.

*Today, children of all races and **ethnicities** learn together in Virginia schools.*

Virginia's Achievers

Arthur Ashe Jr.

Ashe, Arthur R. Jr. (1943–1993), athlete. Arthur Ashe was a world-champion, African-American tennis player. He fought against **prejudice** in an all-white tennis world. In 1980, he retired from tennis. He had contracted **AIDS** from blood transfusions during a heart surgery. Despite his illness, Arthur Ashe continued to work hard to end **discrimination.** His book, *Hard Road to Glory,* is a history of African-American athletes.

Bacon, Nathaniel (1647–1676), soldier. Nathaniel Bacon led an attack on Native Americans in Virginia in the 1670s. The governor of the Virginia colony declared Bacon an outlaw. Bacon then marched on Jamestown and took over the government for two months. Bacon believed he was fighting for the rights of Virginians. His fight became known as Bacon's Rebellion.

Nathaniel Bacon

Bailey, Pearl (1918–1990), entertainer. Born in Newport News, Pearl Bailey became a famous African-American singer and entertainer. She performed on stage, in the movies, and on television. She won a Tony award in 1967 for her performance in the musical *Hello, Dolly.* In 1975, Pearl Bailey was appointed to the United Nations as a goodwill **ambassador.**

Beatty, Warren (b. 1937), actor. Warren Beatty grew up in northern Virginia. Beatty and his sister, actress Shirley MacLaine, graduated from Washington Lee High School in Arlington. Beatty worked as a rat catcher in a Virginia movie theater before appearing on the movie screens himself as an actor. Beatty has appeared in more than twenty films. He has won two Academy Awards for best director.

Warren Beatty

Braxton, Carter (1736–1797), signer of the Declaration of Independence. Carter Braxton was elected to the **House of Burgesses** in 1765. He served in the **Continental Congress** from 1774 until 1776, and was elected to the Virginia General Assembly two times.

Byrd, Harry F. Sr. (1887–1966), politician. Harry F. Byrd was born in Winchester. Byrd served in the Virginia General Assembly as a senator from 1915 to 1925. He was then elected as governor in 1926. He served as a United States senator from Virginia from 1933 until 1965. Harry Byrd started the "Pay As You Go" idea for a gasoline tax to pay for state roads. He also started the massive resistance movement in the 1950s, during which some people refused to obey **integration** laws.

Harry F. Byrd Sr.

Byrd, Richard E. (1888–1957), explorer. Richard Byrd, the brother of Harry Byrd Sr., was also born in Winchester. As a pilot and explorer, he was the first person to fly over both the North and South Poles. He also explored Antarctica.

Cather, Willa (1873–1947), writer. Willa Cather was born in Virginia. She wrote books about her memories of Virginia and the Nebraska prairie, where she later moved. She won the **Pulitzer Prize** in 1923 for the novel *One of Ours*.

Clark, George Rogers (1752–1818), frontiersman, soldier. George Rogers Clark was born in Shadwell. He was the older brother of William Clark (see below). George was a **frontier** fighter during the Revolutionary War (1775–1783). He helped win the western frontier in the Ohio River Valley from Great Britain.

William Clark

Clark, William (1770–1838), soldier, explorer. William Clark was born in Caroline County. Together with Meriwether Lewis, Clark served as a member of the **militia** against the Native Americans of the Ohio Valley in 1789. He was hired to explore the Louisiana Territory with Lewis in 1803. After the big trip, Clark became superintendent of Indian affairs in St. Louis. Then, in 1813, he became governor of the Missouri Territory.

Cline, Patsy (1932–1963), singer. As a country-music singer from Winchester, Cline won many honors, including recognition in the Country Music Hall of Fame, the Recording Hall of Fame, and the National Cowgirl Hall of Fame.

Couric, Katie (b. 1957), journalist. A popular and respected morning news show host, Katie Couric was born in Arlington. She began her career with reporting and producing jobs for NBC stations in Miami, Florida, and Washington, D.C. Couric joined the NBC Network News in 1989. She has been co-anchor of NBC's *Today Show* since 1991.

Katie Couric

Rita Dove

Dove, Rita (b. 1952), poet. Born in Akron, Ohio, Rita Dove became a professor of English at the University of Virginia in 1989. She has won many awards, including the **Pulitzer Prize** for poetry in 1987. In 1993, she was named the **Poet Laureate** of the United States. She was the first African American to hold that post. Rita Dove lives in Charlottesville.

Ella Fitzgerald

Fitzgerald, Ella (1918–1996), singer. Ella Fitzgerald was born in Newport News. She was a great African-American jazz singer, and was known as the "First Lady of Song." Fitzgerald won ten Grammy awards for her performances.

Glasgow, Ellen (1873–1945), writer. Ellen Glasgow grew up in Richmond. She began writing books when she was only seven years old. Glasgow learned by reading and traveling. Glasgow won many awards for writing, including the Pulitzer Prize for fiction in 1942. She wrote about life in Virginia and how it was changing. She also challenged the **traditional** ideas of a woman's role in society.

Harrison, William Henry (1773–1841), U.S. president. Harrison was the ninth president of the United States. He was born in Charles City County, Virginia, but lived most of his life in Ohio. He became famous in the wars against Native Americans in 1811. He defeated the British at the Battle of Tippecanoe Creek. Harrison became president of the United States in 1840, but contracted pneumonia and died one month after he took office.

Patrick Henry

Henry, Patrick (1736–1799), governor. Patrick Henry was one of Virginia's leaders during the Revolutionary War (1775–1783). He was a famous **patriot** who spoke out against the British **Stamp Act.** In 1776, Patrick Henry became the first elected governor of Virginia. He was reelected in 1784 to serve for two more years. He refused to support the first U.S. Constitution. He was afraid that individual states would lose their power. Patrick Henry is most often remembered for his speech favoring American independence from Britain, in which he said, "Give me liberty, or give me death."

Jackson, General Thomas "Stonewall" (1824–1863), soldier. Thomas Jackson was born in Clarksburg. He attended the U.S. Military Academy at West Point and later fought in the Mexican War (1846–1848). He was teaching at the Virginia Military Institute when the Civil War began in 1861. He became a general and fought with the Confederate army. He earned the nickname "Stonewall" at the Battle of Bull Run at Manassas. When troops began to retreat, Jackson urged his troops forward. Another general, Barnard Bee, shouted, "There stands Jackson like a stone wall...rally behind the Virginian boys!" In May 1863, Jackson was accidentally shot by his own men.

Jefferson, Thomas (1743–1826), statesman, governor, U.S. president. Thomas Jefferson was an **architect,** a writer, a scientist, and a leader for the new U.S. government. Although he accomplished much, Thomas Jefferson asked for only the following to be carved on his tombstone: "Here was buried Thomas Jefferson, author of the Declaration

Thomas Jefferson

of American Independence, of the Statute of Virginia for Religious Freedom, and father of the University of Virginia."

Lee, Henry (1756–1818), soldier, statesman. Henry Lee was born at Leesylvania near Dumfries, Virginia. Lee was a **cavalry** officer in the Continental Army, where he earned the nickname "Light Horse Harry." In 1792, he was elected governor of Virginia. Henry Lee was the father of Civil War general Robert E. Lee.

Lee, Francis Lightfoot (1734–1797), signer of the Declaration of Independence. Francis Lightfoot Lee was born to a wealthy family in Loudon County, Virginia. He served in the Virginia **House of Burgesses** at the time the colonies were arguing against the Stamp Act. In 1775, he was sent to the **Continental Congress** as a Virginia **delegate.** He supported the movement for freedom, and signed the Declaration of Independence in 1776.

Lee, Richard Henry (1732–1794), signer of the Declaration of Independence. Richard Henry Lee was only 25 years old when he was elected to the Virginia House of Burgesses. He was the first Virginian to speak out for independence from Britain. He introduced the resolution for independence in Congress on June 7, 1776. Lee served in the U.S. Senate from 1784 to 1789. He was a brother of Francis Lightfoot Lee.

Lee, Robert E. (1807–1870), general. Robert E. Lee was the son of "Light Horse Harry" Lee. He commanded the Army of Northern Virginia and later the entire Confederate Army in the Civil War (1861–1865). General Robert E. Lee surrendered his army to Ulysses S. Grant at Appomattox Court House on April 9, 1865. After the Civil War, Lee became the president of Washington College in Lexington, Virginia.

*Meriwether
Lewis*

Lewis, Meriwether (1774–1809), explorer. Meriwether Lewis was born in Albemarle County, Virginia. Lewis joined the U.S. army when he was twenty and became a captain. In 1801, he became President Jefferson's personal secretary. Lewis was asked to lead the exploration of the Louisiana Territory in 1803. He invited William Clark to help him. After the successful **expedition,** he was made governor of the Louisiana Territory in 1807.

Madison, James (1751–1836), U.S. president. James Madison was the fourth U.S. president. He is known as the "Father of the U.S. Constitution." He was the author of the Virginia Plan, which said states should have equal votes in Congress. James Madison also helped write the Bill of Rights.

James Madison

Marshall, John (1755–1833), chief justice. John Marshall was born on the **frontier** of Fauquier County. He was elected as a representative to the U.S. Congress in 1799, but became secretary of state in 1800. Marshall was most famous for his work as the fourth chief justice of the Supreme Court. He felt that the Supreme Court should decide whether or not the Constitution is violated in specific cases.

Mason, George (1725–1792), **diplomat.** George Mason was the author of the Virginia Declaration of Rights. He also helped write the first Virginia Constitution. Mason was a member of the Virginia **House of Burgesses** before the American

George Mason

Revolution (1775–1783), and he voted for independence from Britain. After the war, he wrote a paper called the Fairfax Resolves, and his ideas became the Virginia Declaration of Rights in 1776, were part of Virginia's state first laws, and eventually were added to the U.S. Constitution as part of the Bill of Rights.

Maury, Matthew Fontaine (1806–1873), scientist, naval officer. Matthew F. Maury was born near Fredericksburg, Virginia, but grew up in Tennessee. He joined the navy and sailed around the world. While he was in the navy, he studied ocean currents and charted the course of the **Gulf Stream.** He also drew maps explaining the currents and winds of the sea. Maury published the first textbook of modern **oceanography,** titled *The Physical Geography of the Sea.* He was called the Pathfinder of the Seas.

McCormick, Cyrus (1809–1884), inventor. Cyrus McCormick grew up in the Shenandoah Valley. Valley farmers grew a large amount of wheat and harvested it all by hand. Cyrus McCormick invented a reaper, which is a grain cutting machine that helped farmers harvest crops faster than by hand.

McGuffey, William H. (1800–1873), educator, writer. William McGuffey was a professor at the University of Virginia. He was the author of the *McGuffey Readers,* which were books used by schoolchildren all over the United States. McGuffey sold 122 million copies of his readers.

James Monroe

Monroe, James (1758–1831), U.S. president. James Monroe was the fifth president of the United States. He believed that European countries should leave North and South America alone. His Monroe Doctrine was a policy that said Europe could no longer invade the Western Hemisphere to start new colonies.

Pocahontas

Pocahontas (ca. 1595–1617), Native American princess. Pocahontas was the daughter of Chief Powhatan of the Algonquin Indians in the Tidewater region of Virginia. Although her real name was Matoaka, she is better known as Pocahontas, which means "Little Wanton," or playful little girl. Pocahontas befriended John Smith and the other British colonists who had arrived here. She brought food to the Jamestown settlers when they were starving. Later, Pocahontas was kidnapped and taken to the settlement at Henricus, near present-day Richmond. She learned to read and became a **Christian.** She took a new name, Rebecca, and married John Rolfe in Jamestown in 1614. In 1616, she gave birth to a baby son, Thomas.

Poe, Edgar Allan (1809–1849), writer. Poe was born in Massachusetts, but lived in Richmond, Virginia. He went to the University of Virginia and the United States Military Academy. He is most famous for his scary stories and poetry, such as "The Tell-Tale Heart" and "The Raven."

Joseph Jenkins Roberts

Roberts, Joseph Jenkins (1809–1876), president of Liberia. Joseph J. Roberts was born a free African American in Norfolk, and moved to Petersburg when he was a child. He worked in his family's **import/ export** business. Roberts and his family moved to the new African colony of Liberia in 1829. He became governor there and was later elected president of Liberia.

Robinson, Bill "Bojangles" (1878–1949), entertainer. Born in Richmond, Bill "Bojangles" Robinson was famous worldwide for his tap dancing. His parents died when he was a small child. He learned to dance on the

Bill "Bojangles" Robinson

streets of Richmond. He left Richmond and went to Washington, D.C., to make a living by dancing. He became famous when he appeared in several movies with actress Shirley Temple.

Scott, Willard (b. 1934), weather reporter. Willard Scott was born in Arlington, but his career as the weather reporter for NBC's *Today Show* has taken him all around the world. Scott was the first to play the character of Ronald McDonald, and he has also been seen by millions as the anchor of the Macy's Thanksgiving Day parade in New York City. Scott has been honored numerous times, including being named Distinguished Virginian by the Virginia Association of Broadcasters (1990) and being recognized by President Ronald Reagan with the Private Sector Award for Public Service in 1985.

Shepard, Alan B. (1923–1998), astronaut. Alan B. Shepard was the first U.S. astronaut in space. He was living in Virginia Beach at the time he flew on *Mercury 3* on May 5, 1961. He reached an **altitude** of 116 miles on that trip and left the force of gravity. Ten years later in 1971, Shepard commanded *Apollo 14* and walked on the moon for nine hours.

Alan Shepard

Smith, Captain John (1580–1631), explorer, soldier, mapmaker. Smith was a British soldier hired by the London Company. In 1607, he was part of the first group of colonists in Jamestown. He was president of the Virginia Colony from 1608 to 1609. Smith wrote a book about his adventures called *Generall Historie of Virginia*. His maps of the locations of Virginia's Native Americans at that time are still helpful to **archaeologists** today.

Snead, Sam (1912–2002), professional golfer. Sam Snead of Hot Springs was a champion athlete. He won both the Masters and Professional Golfers' Association (PGA) tournaments three times and the British Open once. Snead was the runner-up in the U.S. Open four times and the PGA Player of Year in 1949. In 1965, he became the oldest player, at 52 years and 10 months, to win a PGA event. Snead is currently the all-time PGA Tour career victory leader, with 81 wins.

Spotswood, Alexander (1676–1740), royal governor. In 1716, Spotswood led a group of explorers over the Blue Ridge Mountains and claimed new lands for King George I. He named the friends who traveled with him "The Knights of the Golden Horseshoe."

Jeb (James Ewell Brown) Stuart

Stuart, General James Ewell Brown (1833–1864), soldier. "Jeb" Stuart was one of the Confederate army's best **cavalry** officers. General Robert E. Lee called him "the eyes of the army." Stuart was wounded near Richmond on May 10, 1864, and died two days later.

Taylor, Zachary (1784–1850), U.S. president. Zachary Taylor, nicknamed Old Rough and Ready, was born near Barboursville, Virginia. He was a successful general during the Mexican War (1846–1848) and became a popular hero. Taylor became the twelfth president of the United States in 1848.

Turner, Nat (1800–1831), slave leader. Nat Turner was a slave who led a **revolt** in Southampton County, Virginia, in 1831. He believed that God told him to lead his people to freedom. He led more than 60 slaves against **plantation** owners and their families. The Virginia **militia** was called in to stop the revolt. Nat Turner was captured, tried, and hanged for leading the revolt.

Tyler, John (1800–1831), U.S. president. John Tyler was the tenth president of the United States, from 1841 to 1845. Tyler spent most of his life as a lawmaker. He was in the Virginia General Assembly and was a governor of Virginia. He was also vice president to William Henry Harrison. When Harrison died in 1841, Tyler became president.

Valentine, Lila Meade (1865–1921), activist. Lila Meade Valentine lived in Richmond all of her life. She became nationally known for working for women's **suffrage.** Valentine was one of the first women in Richmond to vote in an election. She also worked to improve public education and public health in Virginia.

Washington, Booker T. (1856–1915), educator. Booker T. Washington was born a slave. As a free man after the Civil War, he worked his way through school by doing many jobs. Upon graduating from Hampton Institute, Booker T. Washington became a teacher. He later worked at a school in Alabama named Tuskegee Institute that helped freed slaves. Washington believed that the way to freedom was through education.

Washington, George (1732–1799), soldier, statesman, U.S. president. George Washington was commander in chief of the American army during the Revolutionary War (1775–1783). Before that he was a British soldier in the French and Indian War (1754–1763). He led American **patriots** to victory and independence from Britain. Washington became the first president of the United States in 1789 and was called the Father of the Country.

George Washington

White, John (ca. 1540–ca. 1593), explorer, artist. In 1585, an English explorer named John White visited Native Americans in what are now North Carolina and Virginia and drew pictures of their **cultures.** His drawings and paintings are some of the only original pictures of Algonquin Indian culture.

Wilder, L. Douglas (b. 1931), governor. Lawrence Douglas Wilder was born in Richmond. Wilder entered the U.S.

Army, fought in the Korean War, and won the Congressional Medal of Honor for bravery during combat. He then went to law school and became a lawyer. In 1989, Wilder became the governor of Virginia, the first African American to be elected governor of any state.

Wilson, Woodrow (1856–1924), U.S. president. Wilson was born in Staunton, Virginia, but grew up in Georgia and South Carolina. From 1902 to 1910, he served as president of Princeton University. Wilson was the 28th president of the United States, and he led the United States through World War I (1914–1918). He was one of the founders of the **League of Nations.**

Woodrow Wilson

Woodson, Carter Godwin (1875–1950), publisher. Carter Woodson was born in New Canton. He was the son of a former slave. He started high school when he was twenty years old and went on to earn a doctorate degree from Harvard University in 1912. Woodson started a publishing company in 1920 to help preserve the history of African Americans.

Wythe, George (1726–1806), statesman, teacher. George Wythe was the first law professor at the College of William and Mary in Williamsburg. Thomas Jefferson was one of his students. Wythe was a member of the Virginia **House of Burgesses.** He also signed the Declaration of Independence. Wythe was against slavery and freed his slaves before he died.

George Wythe

Map of Virginia

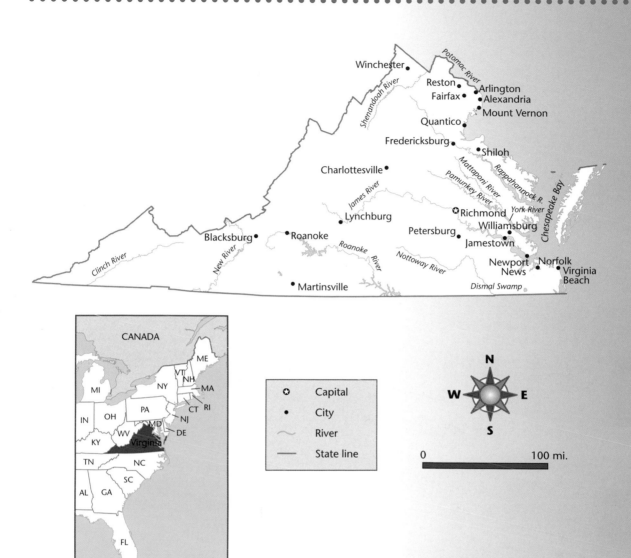

Winchester

Potomac River

Reston
Fairfax
Arlington
Alexandria
Mount Vernon

Quantico

Fredericksburg
Shiloh

Shenandoah River

Charlottesville

Mattaponi River
Rappahannock R.
Pamunkey River

James River

Richmond
York River

Lynchburg
Petersburg
Williamsburg

Chesapeake Bay

Blacksburg
Roanoke
Jamestown

Roanoke River

Newport
News
Norfolk
Virginia
Beach

Clinch River

New River

Nottoway River

Dismal Swamp

Martinsville

CANADA

ME
VT
NH
NY
MA
MI
CT
RI
PA
NJ
IN
OH
MD
DE
WV
KY
Virginia
TN
NC
SC
AL
GA
FL

✪	Capital
•	City
∼	River
—	State line

N
W   E
S

0   100 mi.

Glossary

agricultural having to do with farming

AIDS Acquired Immunodeficiency Syndrome. A condition caused by a virus that leads to a dangerous illness, and usually death

Allies nations that sided with France and England in World War I

altitude height above the earth's surface

ambassador person sent as a representative or messenger

archaeologist person who studies history through the things that people have made or built

architect person who designs buildings and gives advice on their construction

artisan person who makes crafted products like glass or silverware

bade commanded or asked

cavalry soldiers who are trained to fight on horseback

census count of population and the gathering of information about that population

Christian person who believes in the teachings of Jesus

commerce buying and selling goods

Continental Congress group of people who spoke and acted on behalf of the people of the colonies which later became the United States of America

county seat town that is the head of the administration for the area

courtesy polite act or remark

culture ideas, skills, arts, and a way of life of a certain people at a certain time

debt owing to another

delegate give a right or duty to another

Democrat member of the Democratic Party, one of two main political groupings in the United States

depression time when businesses are doing poorly

descendant/descent child or children of ancestors

diplomat someone who works to maintain relations between governments of different countries

discrimination unfair treatment of people based on their differences from others

diverse/diversity having variety

economy control of money that is earned and spent in a home, business, or government

Emancipation Proclamation ruling issued by U.S. President Abraham Lincoln on January 1, 1863, that freed the slaves of the Confederate states that rebelled against the Union

equality condition of being the same, especially in political, social, and economic rights and duties

ethnic belonging to a group with a particular culture

exiled banished or sent out from one's country

expedition organized journey of exploration with a group of people

export send goods out of one country to another

fall line line of small waterfalls and rapids In Virginia

famine time when food is scarce and people are starving

fertile bearing crops or vegetation in abundance

fort strong building used for defense again an enemy attack

frontier edge of the wilderness

Great Wagon Road route of commerce and travel between Pennsylvania, Delaware, Maryland, and Virginia

Gulf Stream warm ocean current flowing northeastward in the North Atlantic

guncotton explosive substance used for smokeless powder

House of Burgesses representative assembly in colonial Virginia

Ice Age period of colder climate when much of North America was covered by thick glaciers

immigrant person who moves permanently into a new country to live

import bring goods from one country to another

indentured servant person who signed a contract agreeing to work in exchange for passage to Virginia

industry/industrial any kind of business, trade, or manufacturing

integrate bring together into a whole

land bridge land connecting Alaska and Siberia during the last Ice Age

League of Nations first international organization set up to maintain world peace

legacy something handed down through the generations

Louisiana Purchase western half of the Mississippi River basin purchased in 1803 from France by the United States

metropolitan area surrounding a large city

militia group of citizens who serve as soldiers

oceanography the study of the ocean regions

ore rock or mineral from which a metal can be obtained

passage passenger space, especially on a ship

patriot person who loves and supports his or her country

persecution continual treatment in a way meant to be cruel and harmful

plantation large farm in the South for growing crops like tobacco

poet laureate official poet of a state or country

prejudice unfair opinion formed without careful thought

Presbyterian form of church government developed by Swiss and Rhineland Reformers during the 16th century

Protestant most Christian denominations that are not Roman Catholic or Eastern Orthodox

Pulitzer Prize award given in the United States in several fields, including literature, education, and public service

reservation public land set aside for use by Native Americans

revolt rebel against authority

secede leave a political union

segregation setting one type of people apart from others

Stamp Act first British attempt to raise money by direct taxation of colonial goods

suffrage the right to vote

textile cloth or fabric

toleration respecting the beliefs and practices of others

tradition/traditional custom or belief handed down from generation to generation

tribute something that is given, done, or said to show thanks or respect

Underground Railroad system of cooperation by antislavery people in the United States before 1863 by which runaway slaves were secretly helped to reach freedom

unity together as one

More Books to Read

• •

Coleman, Brooke. *The Colony of Virginia*. New York: Powerkids Press, 2000.

Issacs, Sally Senzell. *America in the Time of George Washington, 1747 to 1803*. Des Plaines, Ill.: Heinemann Library, 1998.

Mellow, Tara. *John Smith*. Philadelphia, Penn.: Chelsea House Publishers, 1999.

Index

About the Author

Karla Smith grew up in a navy family and moved several times before settling down in Suffolk, Virginia. She has been teaching third, fourth, and fifth graders social studies since 1969. When she is not teaching, Smith enjoys exploring Virginia's waters in a sailboat.